Don't Sell Me, Tell Me

How to use **storytelling** to connect
with the hearts and wallets of a hungry audience.

Greg Koorhan

ISBN-13: 978-0692748275 paperback
ISBN-10: 069274827X

Published by Crossbow Studio

CrossbowStudio.com

Dedicated to my wife, Terry, and my incredible children Leo and Sophie, who consistently and unwaveringly support every one of my crazy ideas. I love each of you with all my heart. And then some.

As a huge thank you for reading *Don't Sell Me, Tell Me*, I've created a workbook for you to use as you go though the exercises. Probably a good idea to download it now, so you'll have it handy.

It will help you find your most powerful brand voice and structure stories so that your most profitable audience becomes eager and ready to hear from you.

Go ahead. I'll wait here.

http://dontsellmetellmebook.com/member/

Contents

Introduction

Every business owner wants to stand out in their market and yet most all suffer in crippling obscurity. To their potential customers, they all sound the same. There is nothing different about their marketing message. They don't have a unique brand. They spend money on advertising, they re-do their logo or their website, and still they cannot seem to get attention.

But there is a book that shows you how to rise above the sea of me-too competition and build a strong, memorable brand that customers know, like and trust. *Don't Sell Me, Tell Me* has been designed to help you quickly communicate your unique value - to your desired audience - and gather a loyal group of fans eager to buy from you. This book is for business owners and entrepreneurs who are tired of being the 'best kept secret' in their market.

With more than 30 years of helping local, national and international companies develop marketing campaigns that cut through the clutter and grow their businesses, I've faced similar themes and uncovered common pitfalls. Then as an award-winning filmmaker and writer, I've been honing the craft of distilling the honest, the unique and the interesting out of everyday experiences.

Entrepreneurs who know they have something to offer and yet struggle with getting clients to notice will find this helpful guide a refreshing shortcut to getting their message to connect, in a meaningful way, with their ideal customers and rebuild trust in their brand.

This is not a book about picking new colors or redesigning your logo. This is not another book on marketing tricks or secret hacks. In fact, it eschews most of what businesses practice today.

Clients and students have described this approach as "full of pragmatic advice distilled into a manner I could put to use right away. I look at my marketing entirely differently now and the effect was immediate!"

We promise that if you follow the straightforward steps in this guide, your marketing will be 10X more effective and you'll build a brand that stands apart from your competitors — to the point where your ideal customers will actually seek you out. You'll connect with your most profitable audience on a level you never have before.

You can continue to say the same things, putting out the same type of marketing messages you (and all your competitors) have been doing, with spotty, unremarkable results. Or you can choose to follow a process that only a few leaders in their markets have figured out. All you have to do to stand out in your market is to keep reading. The chapters that follow will give you new insights and a clear path to building a unique and memorable brand that attracts a growing audience of eager buyers.

You can do this. Actually, everyone can. But most won't make the effort. It's easier to keep lying to themselves.

It's time to stop wishing someone will notice you and take control over how strongly your brand message connects with your market.

It's time to tell a better story.

Stop the Spinning

Once Upon a Time

Once upon a time it was simple for a business to connect with its customers. If you owned a business, most likely it was local. You knew your customers personally because you saw them every day. You knew their families and where they lived. You knew what made them happy, you knew their struggles and they knew yours. They liked doing business with you; they knew your story and what you stood for. They were loyal to you and you to them. Today, that sounds like a fairytale in an imaginary town.

Today, even though every business still needs to connect with its customers, that's easier said than done. It's not news that we are all being bombarded with so many advertising messages and sales pitches that it would make previous generations' heads spin. Speaking louder or more often is not the answer. With enough money, a business can get in front of almost any consumer. The problem has become how to get them to pay attention.

The job of effective marketing has always been to create the right message for the right audience, and deliver it through the right medium at the right time. That, at its core, still holds true. And over the course of this book we are going to look at each of those components: the message, the audience, the medium and the timing. But we're going to start by showing you how to transcend a bad habit that is epidemic in the marketing of businesses big and small.

Simply, over the years much of marketing and positioning has gotten a bad rap because of "spin." Remember the fairytale where they try to spin straw into gold? Spin in marketing is the modern day attempt to do the same. Only now companies try to spin a commodity product into something special. Spin a poor service into something that is desirable. Spin a poor relationship into a loyal customer.

This has been going on for years. As I said, epidemic. And yet it's not working. Over time, more and more consumers have grown to see through this veil. We've all grown weary of inauthentic marketing messages and sales hype. The majority of advertising has become noise, the majority of hype we don't believe, most of the rest we just ignore.

Most.

There are some messages, from a small number of companies, that get through. And these companies enjoy the type of following that the rest only dream of. Their audiences stay connected and loyal. Their customers wait in anticipation for news of what's next.

What makes them so special? What makes them unique?

Not So Unique

This may seem obvious, but no business stands out by being just like all the rest of their competition. Yet, what most businesses think is a unique selling proposition is just using the same tired phrases and marketing jargon that every other company in their industry uses.

If you've been in business for any length of time, you've probably heard companies talk of their people, their process and their technology as if that's what makes them different. News flash: every business has people, processes and technology. I can't even tell you the number of consultants that I've heard pitch their 'unique' combination of their strategy, their creativity and their technology. And since they are consultants, there is usually a Venn diagram along with it. As if that somehow makes them different from every other consultant that combines strategy, creativity and technology.

Worse are the companies that use jargon to describe what they do. Using jargon in your marketing is just being lazy. It's like talking to yourself. Most of it is acronyms and phrases that the consumer doesn't care about or understand anyway. So it has the opposite effect, confusing the very people they are trying to reach, putting up yet another barrier to the sale.

It's called corporate speak. Don't use it.

The biggest problem with corporate speak is that it smacks of trying to sound like everyone else, as if that makes you more legit, more credible. The result, however, is the opposite. Using these phrases that don't mean anything to the audience, only meaning something to the corporations that are trying to sound smarter, in fact distances the company from its audience.

So your first step in creating a better connection with your audience is to dump the corporate speak, the jargon, and the tired phrases every company in your industry has been using. The next step is to recognize another "elephant in the room" — that is, it's not an effective message when the only one believing it is the one telling it.

Seeing through the Veil

Early on, there was a degree of trust in the media, and marketing messages were given the benefit of the doubt. But after years of both undifferentiated corporate speak and marketing hype, not so much. It's evident customers just see through the current rash of marketing spin.

Take a look at the two largest consumer groups today: Baby Boomers and Millennials. Baby Boomers grew up in the days depicted in the television show *Mad Men*. Advertising in that day reflected society's desires, striving for an ideal future, painting a picture of the American dream. But after decades of buying too many products that didn't deliver on that dream, baby boomers have had enough. They've simply put up with it for too long. They are looking for something more authentic.

Millennials, on the other hand, never really bought the "way it always has been." They grew up questioning, a little distrustful of the establishment. "It's always been that way" was never a good enough reason. It may be because they're more in touch with what is important to them. Or it may be that they've decided that there's a better way, but in either case the veil of spin marketing doesn't cut it anymore for this group either.

For both population sets, pulling back the curtain exposes the barrage of messages that at minimum don't help a company stand out from the crowd, and at worst exposes a massive disconnect with what the company is doing and what they are saying.

And that brings us to the third and arguably the most important step: walking the talk.

The Big Incongruency

Every business says they want to be unique. But it seems that, more often than not, they act the opposite. They say they want to be dynamic but they use cautious words and bland imagery. They say they want to be creative, but they don't want to try an idea unless it's been done before. They want to stand out and sound different but they use the same language that everyone else uses.

Or, if they do take a stand and position themselves as something more dynamic in their marketing materials, it's incongruent with how they actually act, internally or as a corporate citizen. We've all done it, if not in business, then in our personal lives. It's really not anybody's fault. It's not easy to do in the first place. It's like eating right or exercising — we know what has to be done. We know it's good for us and yet we still sneak that chocolate bar whenever we can.

I've done it. Heck, I still do it. Struggling with incongruence is an issue everyone has at one point or another. But when our words and actions don't align, it makes everything else harder. Even if we, by some chance, come up with a distinctive message, not acting in alignment with that message makes it less believable. Again, the net effect is that the only ones we are fooling are ourselves.

Have you ever been on hold with a company, while listening to a voice recording loop over and over, telling you how important you are to them? How important can you really be to them if they keep you waiting forever to answer your questions?

Okay, so if, as business owners we all know that not "walking the talk" is a bad idea, why do we still do it? Why do we continually present one face to the public in our marketing, and another in our actions — and at the same time tell ourselves this is effective marketing communication? You can rationalize, you can call it denial, but we are simply lying, at least to ourselves.

DON'T SELL ME, TELL ME

"What do you mean, lying?," you say. "I'm not a liar!"

Not intentionally, anyway. Nobody thinks of themselves as a liar so let's talk about that for a moment: why do we lie?

Who Are We Lying To, Anyway?

Lying to Others

When we use the word "lying" it conjures up an image of an intentionally false or deceitful practice - trying to "pull the wool over someone's eyes" for personal gain. Emphasis on the word "intentional." In business, and in life, actually, I believe that people are generally good and would rather do the right thing. Most people don't start a business for the purpose of deceiving the public.

But we're human, and there are a couple of scenarios when we don't always do the right thing.

The first is to avoid looking bad.

For instance, we've all seen cases where a mistake has been made and rather than owning up to the mistake it gets covered up. And that's where the trouble starts.

The mistake — unless it's a life or death situation — is just that, a mistake. It's usually not a problem that cannot be overcome. It might be uncomfortable when working through it, but it can be cleaned up. The real problem is when the company or its leadership doesn't own up to and take responsibility for the mistake. Or worse, they intentionally try to cover it up. Then they start stacking lies on top of lies just to avoid looking bad.

This type of lying always gets uncovered, and at that point a bigger problem arises — a lack of trust. In trying not to look bad, they've made the situation worse. Because lack of trust is a problem that lasts longer and is harder to overcome than the challenge presented by the original mistake in the first place. So, the irony is, while these types of lies come from a fear of judgment, in doing so the perpetrator usually ends up in a worse spot than the one they were trying to avoid.

Telling the truth only when it is non-threatening carries a hidden, psychological cost as well. When avoidance of consequences becomes the priority and we end up only telling the truth when it's convenient, then we must carry around with us an uncomfortable inventory of past censorships.

Stack enough of these on top of one another and it inhibits future decision making. Not a way to build a strong foundation for your business.

Okay, so we know that this definition of lying — the intentional type — is bad. Bad ethically, bad psychologically and bad legally.

I'm going to make the assumption that because you are reading this book, you are a person that wants to be known for telling the truth and wants to build a business and brand you can be proud of.

So let's look at another type of lying that can be just as crippling to you and your business. Not an intentional "fib," as in the scenario we just discussed; in this lie we perpetuate false statements because we don't know the truth ourselves. It stands to reason that you cannot share the truth if you're not aware of it. Sometimes it's easy to overlook or avoid a fact than to it is to face it.

Why take the time — we subconsciously challenge ourselves — to examine a question if we would rather not know the answer?

This is something that trips up many businesses and can undermine the trust in your brand without you really knowing it, so let's look at that next.

Lying to Ourselves

Quite simply, if we are not looking deep enough, if we are avoiding a truth, we are lying to ourselves.

This is not a judgment. It's not your fault.

Everybody does it. Avoiding the uncomfortable is a protection mechanism. It's natural to be afraid of being vulnerable or of showing weakness. It's something that's in our DNA and it's been that way for thousands and thousands of years, ever since we hunted for food. You can still see it in animal herds. If you show vulnerability, you can become a target. In a bad way.

Being singled out from the herd in that way means you become prey to any nearby predators.

And since nobody wants to become prey, taking the time or effort to expose your own vulnerabilities is definitely not a priority. In fact, the opposite has become true. Human beings have developed the "skill" to try to "protect themselves" from any vulnerability — without even thinking about it.

We lie to ourselves, because to do otherwise would be to admit we actually have vulnerabilities.

So if, instinctually, exposing weakness is dangerous — why would anyone blame you? When you extrapolate that a form of weakness is the feeling of embarrassment or judgment, it's perfectly understandable to try to save face.

It's a built in mechanism to try and "be accepted" — to be liked or to fit in. Again, perfectly understandable.

Another way of drawing negative attention is when we stand out — usually because of something we've done or said. We might also be afraid that we're going to offend someone, turn them off or make them stop liking us. This viewpoint is often used to shape marketing messages — "keep it politically correct" — yet it's just as often something we tell ourselves instead of looking past that at the real reason. The real reason is probably not because we'll offend, or make the recipient feel bad, it's the reaction we may get that we fear.

It's actually, again, a fear that we won't be liked, or that we'll be singled out.

You cannot please everyone all of the time. And when you try to be liked by everyone, the result is usually being truly liked by no one.

A less obvious reason we don't put ourselves out there, is because we aren't sure what we'll get in return. Picture a classroom full of schoolchildren trying hard to avoid eye contact with the teacher for fear of being called on. We'd rather avoid dealing with the attention.

Standing out from your competition will logically draw interaction. And what if you don't like the interaction?

Sometimes you don't want to ruin a perfectly good but very superficial relationship by inviting a conversation. After all, if you boldly state your position it's only equitable that you allow the other person to state theirs.

And what are the risks to that? You might get feedback which conflicts with your view. You might get criticized. You might get called out even further. But when we consciously or unconsciously hide behind that fear, we also lose the ability to create a deeper relationship.

All of this is unconscious, remember. It's built in, natural, and perfectly understandable.

Take a step back and think about it, however, and you'll see that no matter how much we worry, fret or fear, we cannot control how somebody will hear or respond to what we are saying. We can only control how we speak, not the interpretation or the reaction to it. In fact, by trying to protect or shield or shape the truth, you are instead diminishing the other person, restricting their access to important information and down-playing their potential. If you speak from a place of wanting only the best outcome, chances are they will be able to hear your message in the way it was intended and draw upon their own internal resources to react appropriately.

I guess what I'm saying is don't underestimate your customer. Show your belief in their ability to handle what you offer and give them the opportunity to surprise and delight you with their response.

Telling the truth to ourselves requires awareness and practice. Awareness to look past the instinctual fear and the continuing practice of communication skills to express it in a meaningful way.

Honesty Will Set You Free

The moment we are willing to be honest with ourselves we have at our disposal an incredible opportunity to leapfrog out of the sea of business competitors. How? Well first of all, because only a rare few in business do this, you'll set yourself apart just by trying!

So congratulations! Isn't it nice to know you can come out of this a winner — and we haven't even got to the good part yet!

Second, when you are willing to be honest with yourself, you open yourself up to a much better understanding of the underlying drivers of your business and how you can best serve your ideal customers. That kind of insight is highly valuable and most business owners never get close to discovering it!

And third, honest feeling and emotion are the base building blocks of story. Why is this important?

As you will soon see, using story can connect you with your customers like nothing else.

In this chapter we looked at the major, subconscious forces that cause us to lie to ourselves, and lie to others. So now that we have a good understanding about what's holding us back, let's look at how to break free of them and make the most of moving forward.

Ready?

Engaging with Stories

Why Are Stories So Engaging?

As humans, we have at our disposal a tool that can effectively and efficiently rebuild lost trust and create a meaningful connection between your business, your brand and your audience.

Storytelling.

Storytelling has been around longer than the written word. Before we had books and manuscripts we started with stories. Stories showed us what was important. Stories told us what to avoid. Stories gave us history and context. They helped us learn from mistakes. They showed us what was possible. Stories helped keep traditions alive. Over time they evolved and became entertainment as well. Those that could tell good stories became respected leaders.

For generations, parents have read bedtime stories to children for the same reasons. To pass along values, lessons, morals and traditions.

From an early age, we are predisposed to learning from stories. "Tell me a story" is a familiar phrase to most parents. "Teach me a lesson" is said by no children, nowhere.

We find drama interesting. And knowingly or unknowingly, we search for meaning in every story. We instinctively learn from the morals. We learn from the mistakes of the characters within. Stories can be pure fantasy and we still connect with them. We cannot help but connect with the characters of the stories even when they are in an unbelievable setting. You only need to look at a science fiction novel or a Hollywood adventure to see that this is true.

The characters of a story show us what's possible in ourselves. And if the story is well told, we care about the characters. We want to know what's next, what happens to the characters along their journey and they keep us on the edge of our seats, yearning to know if things work out alright in the end.

When applied to business, however, it's not about ONLY being fantastic and entertaining. Even for an entertainment company.

But Hollywood has figured out some things that business marketers have not. For instance, filmmakers figured out long ago that we, as an audience, identify with broken heroes in stories. Character flaws let us see ourselves and empathize with the hero. You could look at it as if the product — the hero in the story — has flaws, making it easier for an audience to identify and connect with the character. Conversely, Madison

Avenue, over the last 50 years has tried to paint the product with no flaws. They've had to look to other ways to get an audience to care.

Infallible is not very interesting. Think about it; even Superman has kryptonite as a weakness. Facing obstacles creates drama. Drama is naturally interesting to us.

In a little bit, we're going to go deeper into how to make stories work for you.

But for now it's important to know that, innately, we have a craving for stories. So let's take a look at what's going on when we engage with a story.

Thinking and Feeling

We know that we are hard-wired to crave stories. But why?

For you logical minded people, I'm going to throw some science in here.

You see, stories engage multiple parts of the brain. In addition to areas dealing with language and logic, they also activate areas related to sensory stimuli. A study by the Emory Institute in Atlanta in which participants read the novel *Pompeii* by Robert Harris, and then had MRI scans found that the novel's story led to increased activity in the left temporal cortex, which is one area highly associated with language. Makes sense: reading a language activates the language area of the brain.

But here's the interesting part: the book is a thriller, a historical fiction about the real-life eruption of Mount Vesuvius that overwhelmed Pompeii, and was chosen in part because of it's page turning plot and strong narrative line.

The study also found that just thinking about an action triggers the same emotional and sensory areas of the brain that performing the action does.

Consider that for a moment. Reading about an action activates the same areas in the brain as doing the action. A story about feeling good can make you actually feel good. A story about overcoming an obstacle triggers an area in the brain as if you overcame the obstacle. A story about success can make you feel like you are succeeding.

So by telling a story associated with you or your business, you can trigger the emotions that make your customer feel, even for a brief moment, as if they've experienced the same benefit. The benefit of working with you, your product or your service - before they've purchased from you. Assuming it's a good experience, don't you think they'll want more?

Gregory Berns, the lead author of the study, said, "The neural changes that we found associated with physical sensation and movement systems suggest that reading a novel can transport you into the body of the protagonist."

Compare this to what the brain does when it takes in facts and data. When looking at data, the language areas of the brain light up, but not the emotional and sensory areas. These areas are triggered only by stories. This means that your story can engage your audience in ways data can't. In addition to thinking, they're feeling and actually experiencing the story.

A story can get a customer engaged more that any brochure, listing just features and benefits. A story can literally make someone feel the value of working with you.

Stories do what data does not.

Something to Remember

People forget statistics and facts, but they don't forget a good story.

This is especially true if your story conveys a message related to things your audience cares about deeply. According to Jennifer Aaker, Professor of Marketing at Stanford Graduate School of Business, "Stories are 22 times more memorable than facts alone." Further, she says,

"Studies show that we are wired to remember stories much more than data, facts, and figures. However, when data and stories are used together, audiences are moved both emotionally and intellectually."

The benefits of bedtime stories seem to hold true, even as adults.

Think about the last time you listened to a speaker on stage, spilling out a list of facts and figures. Without referring to your notes, it's really hard to recall any of it. But if the speaker weaves in a good story, suddenly you can remember amazing details from the event, days and even weeks later.

Stories have the power to connect our emotions with the logical, making the mundane more interesting. They help us remember the important bits, because they've been connected to other important feelings.

Maya Angelou once said, *"I've learned that people will forget what you said, people will forget what you did, but people will never forget how you made them feel."*

Stories are remembered because they connect to our emotional center.

But there's another way of looking at why stories are memorable, too. A good story stands out.

Amid all of the content clutter of the internet, a story gets attention. Consider for a minute, the many articles you can find online that offer X number of tips for doing something. They're all fairly generic. But every so often you come across a post that weaves a compelling story. Maybe it's how the author stumbled across the tips, or how putting one to use changed something dramatically in their life. You are far more likely to spend the time (even when it's a long article!) and see it through to the end to see what happens. You pay more attention to it, and probably share it too.

In this chapter, we learned why stories are so engaging and memorable. In the next chapter, we're going to look at how to find the story that works best for your company or brand.

Your Story and Your Business

Your Story IS Your Brand

In the previous chapter, we saw why stories are so engaging. The next logical question is: how do you make stories work for your company or brand?

The answer is deceptively simple.

Story relates to a brand in every type of business. Most people buy from professional services companies because they trust the principals. People follow entertainers because they love the celebrity and what they stand for. Witness how quickly the public turns, however, when that individual does something distasteful. People find it hard to separate the entertainment from the entertainer.

Product companies can build an entire following because the people admire the leadership. And if the company isn't built around its leaders and it's built around a brand instead, people become loyal advocates of the company because they know the background story or the mission of the brand. The story builds an aura of trust. The more the brand stays true to its mission, the more the trust grows. And there is an association of quality with that trust.

So as a business owner, your own story should be the first place to look when developing your brand story. My company has worked with start-ups and established organizations, and the brand story always starts with the leadership.

Where you came from, what you went through, where you are going — these are the elements to weave into your story.

This is a little harder than it seems at first, because you have to be honest with yourself. Where companies get into trouble is when they start making things up.

Because what happens when the brand story is incongruent with the leadership? When what they say is different than what they do? That inauthenticity shows up. Just too much energy is needed in a small business to maintain two faces. It takes its toll sooner or later.

Customers will begin to notice — and they will comment, publicly. Trust is lost. Eventually, the employees feel it and morale goes down. The company crumbles from within.

The easiest way to avoid that disconnect, and eventual disintegration of the brand, is also the way to find a story that you'll most likely get behind. In my experience, in every company, big or small, the company's story is tied to the founder's or leader's story. So that's the place to start.

If the CEO is bold and outgoing, the brand tends to be in-your-face; if the founder is thoughtful and eco-conscious, the brand personifies that. Build your brand story out of your own and there will be no need to fake it down the road. Consistency comes naturally!

And in brand building: with consistency, comes strength.

Will this Work for Me?

It's easy to see how this might apply to companies that have or are building established brands.

But the question comes up all the time. "Will this work for me? I'm just a small business," or "I'm an independent contractor, I don't have a brand."

Well, that's really two questions so the answer comes in two parts. I'll address the second part, the "do I really have a brand" part, first. And to do so it's important to remember what a brand is. A brand is not just your logo, or your favorite color. It's not just your website, or your advertising message. A brand is the sum total of all the experiences a customer has with you or your product or company. It is, in effect, your reputation. So, even as an individual, you have a brand.

And like it or not, if you don't consciously cultivate your brand, your customers will do it for you. So it's in your best interest to put in the effort to build a brand you can be proud of.

I can answer the first part, the "will this work for me?" part, in this way: I've worked with large multi-national companies. I've worked with small local non-profits. I've worked with companies with multiple offices, multiple leaders and solo entrepreneurs in startups. In all of them, the true differentiating factor in the brand was closely tied to the story of the company's leadership. So what

I'm about to share with you will apply if you are an entrepreneur. It applies if you're a small business or a consultant. If you're a local business. If you're an author or a speaker. If you're a musician, a filmmaker or an artist.

Story can be used to help build the brand of both product companies and of service companies. Story can even help individual employees inside of larger organizations. I've yet to meet someone who can't benefit from tapping into their story.

Positioning With Story

Story Benefits

How, exactly, can a story benefit you?

As we've seen, a story, at its core, engages a listener and makes a connection. So by default and in its most simplistic form you can use story to connect with your audience. But what kind of connection can you make?

You will build Trust. If it's an honest story, it's a connection that makes you more accessible, more believable. Believability builds trust and we know that people buy from people they know, like and trust, right?

You will touch their Emotions. As we learned earlier, if we're being honest with ourselves, some vulnerability will come out. Vulnerability builds an emotional connection — and people buy on emotion. They may rationalize their purchase on logic, but people buy on emotion.

You become more Interesting. If it's a well-crafted story, it will keep the audience on the edge of their seat. Just like a child listening to a bedtime story and wanting to know what comes next, your customer will be waiting for each communication. When customers welcome each time you share a part of your story, this effectively lowers your overall cost of advertising. It doesn't cost as much when people are asking for the next chapter. Stories can save you money.

You stand out as Unique. Because the story comes from you and you show vulnerability, your story instantly makes you unique. After all, it's your story! No one else can have all the elements that go into your story. It's yours and yours alone. No more agonizing over how to stand out from the competition.

You are Memorable. Telling your story is better than any tagline that you could come up with in an advertising campaign because it communicates more, and is more memorable, while being less sales-y than any promotion can be.

You remain Consistent. If your story comes from you and you live congruent with your story, you create consistency with your brand. You create consistency with your 'corporate' culture. Your employees begin to adopt the story and help you grow. Then, your brand remains consistent with every customer interaction, every touch point. It's reflected in customer service and in your product marketing. Even at networking events your story will help your brand remain clear and strong.

You create Loyalty. We now know how people experience stories, but there is another interesting side effect. Once someone has a positive experience with your story, they get invested. And nobody wants to see their investments fail. Their interests begin to align with yours. People change from passive customer to loyal fan and actually offer support. Deep down, we all want the good guy in the story to win, right?

These kinds of connections just do not happen as efficiently through any other marketing message or channel. Stories create closer connections.

Building trust. Triggering customer emotions. Making you more interesting and unique. Crafting a more memorable and consistent brand. Developing insanely loyal fans. You can clearly see there are multiple ways using stories can benefit you and make your business more profitable. Now let's take a look at the different types of stories you can use.

Types of Stories

There is more than one type of story you can use to build your brand.

Company or Brand Story

This is a story where your company or brand is the central focus. A company story usually involves how the company came into existence and grew to its current state, often told personally by the founder or first employees. Through the company's story, you convey to your audience the values and culture of your company. It also offers many opportunities for you to include the formats, or plots, that we'll discuss later.

The Personal Story

A personal story is a story from someone's life. It could be how they overcame difficulties or how they reached the place where they are today. It could be something as simple as a scene or situation you observed a few days ago that has relevance to your topic and your audience.

Many personal stories involve overcoming difficulties. For example, you might write a story about a time when you couldn't manage your time well. You were always busy and had many things to do, but no free time to do what you enjoyed. This is the setting of the story. You then discovered a very simple and handy technique for managing time better, which helped you get more done and have more time to yourself.

The Product Story

You can tell stories that relate to products. Your story could be how the product was developed, why it came into existence, a problem the product makers had to solve, or how a customer used it in a creative way.

The Customer Story

A customer story is one in which your customer relates somehow to your product or service. This is one of the best types of stories because it emphasizes the benefits of your offering. When people read about another customer's experience with your product or service, they can imagine themselves in the customer's place and understand directly how your products or services can benefit them. Told authentically, these are some of the most powerful stories because they provide social proof — reducing the risk of making a buying decision, because someone else has done it first and benefitted.

A customer story should focus on a common problem your market faces and how one particular customer overcame this problem with your product. For example, if you sell an organization or filing system, you could ask customers to send in their stories about how their work is different, how they are more productive, after they started using your system. Even better, ask them to send in pictures of their newly organized files so that you can illustrate the stories.

The Employee Story
Employee stories are engaging because they take people behind the scenes and add a human element to your business. Your audience gets a glimpse of the inner workings of your company and how every person involved makes a

difference. These stories are also an excellent way to convey your corporate culture.

An employee story might feature a particular team member and how they've improved a product or service, helped the company reach one of its goals, or bent over backwards for a customer in need. It might also be their own history of how and why they came to the company. An employee story is something personal or professional about someone who works for your company and whose values you feel will resonate with your audience.

The Case Study

A case study is a more detailed and researched story of a person, group, activity, event, process or problem. A case study might look something like a detailed retelling of the development of a product, or its application in a specific situation. The main difference between a case study and the other story types we discussed is the thoroughness of it. The case study allows time to explore an issue, and in going deeper, helps to establish your authority in that topic.

After reading this list you may already have some specific ideas of how one of these types of stories would fit your business. Take a moment and write down the topics. Keep the list nearby as you read the next sections, so you can add to it. You may end up using one, two or several of these story types to build your brand. No matter which type of story you use, however, there are a few critical elements that will make the difference between a good, engaging story and an unremarkable one. In the next chapter, we'll look at those, along with a basic structure for you to follow.

DON'T SELL ME, TELL ME

52

What Makes a Good Story?

Once you have a good understanding of how using stories can build your brand, you are probably itching to get into crafting one for your company. Before we get into how to write your story let's talk about what makes a good story.

Structure

Good stories start with structure. Long stories, short stories, even jokes have structure. You wouldn't start a joke with a punchline, would you?

There are loads of brilliant books, courses and workshops on story structure, so I'm not going to repeat their work here. Instead, I'll give you a high level look, with enough insight to apply it to your business. Once you have the basics down, you can choose to study further if you like. Fair enough?

Every story, since theater in ancient Greece, has followed a similar structure. It's also the basic structure of any big Hollywood movie so it should be relatively recognizable to you.

It's the classic mythical structure, described in depth by Joseph Campbell in his book *The Hero with a Thousand Faces*. The framework was later refined by Christopher Vogler, a former Disney writer, in his book, *The Writer's Journey: Mythic Structure For Writers*. Basically, the story unfolds in three acts, and they go like this:

Act One

In Act One, the "old" or current world is described. The main characters and their relationships are established. At some point something happens that confronts the main character (the protagonist or hero). This is called an "inciting incident" and the protagonist's attempt to deal with it leads to a second and more dramatic situation that motivates the hero into action.

This is called the "turning point" and it signals that the world will never be the same for the protagonist. It's usually a crisis because, after all, most people don't make any change unless there is a crisis. (I hope, after reading this book, you don't wait for a crisis to apply this, but that's another story). Act One ends by raising a dramatic question that will be answered at the end of the third act. In novels or films, the dramatic question is something like, "Will he get the girl?" or "Will she catch the killer?"

Act Two

In Act Two is the actual journey. The hero tries to solve the problem introduced in the first act but it's a struggle because, initially he tries to overcome the obstacle with the "old" way of doing things. Each attempt fails because he does not yet have the skills to deal with the "forces of antagonism" and the hero finds himself in ever-worsening situations. The hero must learn a lesson, a new skill, or gain higher sense of awareness so that he can face the fears that were holding him back. In film, the second act is called "rising action." The hero usually cannot achieve this alone, and must be aided by a mentor or ally.

Act Three

In Act Three, the hero makes a decision or faces that fear and succeeds in overcoming the obstacle. Usually, it's an extremely difficult decision. This is where the dramatic question raised in the first act is resolved and the hero returns to the old world, but has, himself, changed. He now has a new outlook and therefore the world looks different than it did before.

And that's it. I'm over-simplifying a bit — there are many nuances and layers that can (and should) be added - but this basic format is all you will need to start. This basic three-act structure was first documented in Aristotle's *Poetics* and has worked continually from the stages of Shakespeare to the Hollywood blockbusters of today.

As you can see, a well-structured story has a clear beginning, middle and end. It is based around conflict and that conflict's resolution. The conflict is what keeps us tuned in and engaged. It provides suspense and anxiety to move the story along. Even if we know it will turn out well for our characters, the resolution of the conflict (called the "climax") at the end of the story gives us a sense of release and triggers positive emotions.

Every company, product, service and individual has a journey like this. In the chapters that follow we're going to learn how to find the most appropriate story for you and your business, but here's a hint: your product or service is most likely the "new way" of looking at things that shows up at the beginning of Act Three.

Barely scratch the surface of any good sales theory and you can see some variation of this structure: Act One: Define the customer's problem. Act Two: Aggravate the customer's problem. Act Three: Provide the solution (your product) and help the customer imagine a 'new world' using the solution.

But we are not going to stop at the surface. We are going to take it deeper and make it much more interesting!

Strength in Structure

If you are not used to setting up stories you may have a tendency to resist structure as being too rigid. It's not an unusual feeling; many writers struggle with it every time they sit down to write. You may already be having thoughts like, "If my story uses the same structure as every other story, how can I be unique?"

If you are having that feeling at this point, my advice is to push through it and for now, give it a try. Rigidity is a point of view. Structure can be the exact opposite of restricting; it can be quite freeing.

Without structure, your story can crumble at any moment, risking your audience's attention or interest. Strong, lasting stories are that way because they have a common structure. It gives us, as the listener, a framework for understanding. It helps build anticipation and ultimately, a greater feeling of satisfaction as the story finishes.

So give it a try. I'm certain you'll soon see that it's structure that holds up and strengthens your story, instead of confining it.

Next, let's take a look at what actually happens within that structure.

Plot

For there to be a story, something's got to happen. Not just a series of random events, because that would not be very interesting. The events in a narrative generally relate to each other. In other words, they happen because of some previous event, or they cause some conflict. Together, these events are called the "Plot."

Plot is a literary term used to describe the events that make up a story or the main part of a story. These events relate to each other in a pattern or a sequence. The flow of a story depends on the organization of events.

If you wrote, "The king died and then the queen died," there is no plot for the story. But by writing, "The king died and then the queen died of grief," you have provided a plot line for your story.

A plot is a causal sequence of events, giving the "why" for the things that happen. The plot helps the listener understand the choices that the characters in the story make. It helps connect with the character.

The way in which the story elements are arranged in the plot depends on the needs of the story. For example, in a mystery or whodunit, the author will withhold the exposition until later in the story.

Tales As Old As Time

Stories from ancient times are only different from those of today in setting and content. What hasn't changed is the storylines or themes. From the first human stories recorded thousands of years ago to the TV drama you watched the other night, these timeless storylines endure.

Why are these storylines so enduring? Because everyone can identify with them. They speak to fundamental emotions that all humans, regardless of culture, understand and experience. To varying degrees, we've all faced similar themes.

Using these classic plots as a starting point for planning your story can help you create something truly effective and emotional for your audience.

In his book, *The Seven Basic Plots*, Christopher Booker analyzed the psychology behind the classic plots, and gave them names. They are:

- Conquering the Monster
- Rags to Riches
- The Quest
- Voyage and Return
- Comedy
- Tragedy
- Rebirth

Let's consider each one and look at some examples to help you get ideas.

Conquering the Monster

Conquering the monster is a familiar storyline if you've ever seen a horror or science fiction movie. It goes all the way back to the first known work of literature, the *Epic of Gilgamesh* from the ancient Sumerian civilization. In it, the hero Gilgamesh goes on a quest where he does battle with a number of monsters.

Video game enthusiasts will recognize this storyline; it's the same format used in many video games, including "Super Mario Brothers."

In a conquering the monster story, the hero goes on a journey that culminates in the defeat of a terrible monster. The odds are stacked against the lowly hero, but through strength, cunning and whatever other virtues and resources are at-hand or found along the way, the hero finally overcomes the monster and kills it.

You've seen this storyline in the biblical David and Goliath story. It's the plot of many classics of literature such as *Beowulf*. It's the basic plot behind *Godzilla, The Terminator,* and the James Bond movies. It's also one of the main themes in superhero comic books.

The secret is that the "monster" doesn't have to be an actual monster. It can be any type of problem or frustration that your audience faces.

One example in marketing is the Allstate "Mayhem" campaign. The character Mayhem is a metaphor for any type of disaster you could face, and you conquer this monster through insurance. Another good example is Nike's "Just Do It" narrative, where athletes overcome the monster (fear of failure, lack of confidence) by "just doing it."

Rags to Riches

The classic story of the American dream is an example of a rags-to-riches story. Imagine the tale of a poor immigrant that finds himself alone on the shores of America, and through hard work and a little luck, pulls himself up by the bootstraps to one day become a billionaire.

You can see this story in the lives of many early 20th century entrepreneurs like Nelson Rockefeller, or in present day authors such as J.K. Rowling. It appears in classic stories like *Cinderella* and Charles Dickens' *David Copperfield*. Films like *Rocky* and *Slumdog Millionaire* are examples of rags-to-riches stories, and it's the story behind many of today's reality TV shows.

Rags-to-riches stories can be used very effectively to tell brand stories, specially if the company starts out as shoestring operation in someone's basement. A recent example is the story of the app

WhatsApp, which was developed by Ukrainian-born Jan Koum while he was on food stamps and sold five years later to Facebook founder Mark Zuckerberg for $19 billion.

The Quest

With the quest, the main character and their entourage set out on a mission to discover some place, person or object. They face obstacles and temptations along the way, all of which they triumph over and then proceed on. This is a popular storyline because it's exciting and keeps people on the edge of their seats, waiting for the next obstacle. The audience travels along with the heroes, experiencing the discovery vicariously through them.

The Arthurian legend of Sir Galahad's quest for the Holy Grail is a classic example of the quest. More modern examples include the Indiana Jones films, *Lord of the Rings*, and many of the Harry Potter books. Alternatively, J.D. Salinger's novel, *Catcher in the Rye*, is the story of an inner quest to find purpose and meaning.

The quest storyline could be used in your search to discover or create a product that solves the problems and hardships that your audience faces.

Voyage and Return

From Homer to Luke Skywalker, human cultures abound with stories about a hero's journey into a strange or dangerous world and final return home. This is a story anyone who has ever ventured away from home geographically, or ventured outside their comfort zone psychologically, can easily understand. It touches a real nerve with people and the eventual homecoming offers an emotional release.

Most of the time, the hero returns home with nothing more than experience.

These stories are particularly popular with children, maybe because the whole world to them is a strange land full of obstacles.

A number of classics fit this mold like Homer's *Odyssey* and Lewis Carroll's *Alice in Wonderland*. Quite a number of fantasy and science fiction stories use this storyline, including *Back To The Future* and the television series *Lost*. *Finding Nemo* is an excellent example, as well as the most famous of voyage and return stories, *The Wizard of Oz*.

When applying this to yourself, voyage and return can be used in a variety of different contexts. In a literal interpretation, you may have made a discovery while traveling that inspired you to come home and develop a service. Product development can be a voyage and return story if it involves venturing outside of your comfort zone. If you offer travel-related products or services, this plot can also fit really well when telling customer stories.

Comedy

Although comedies are funny, not every funny story is a comedy. Here, the term "comedy" is meant in the Shakespearean sense. In a comedy, the plot revolves around some confusion among the characters, which leads to a wide variety of mishaps and eventually resolves when it's cleared up and the characters are set straight.

Most sitcoms use this storyline for their episodes, as do most romances. One mix-up, mistaken identity or misunderstanding can offer many opportunities for humor. Just take a look at any of your favorite comedies in either movies or TV series for an example.

In a comedy, the hero can be the mixed up person in a sane world, or the only sane person in a mixed up world. Most people can identify with being in the latter situation.

Businesses can use the comedy format to reframe a problem into some type of comedic confusion. A business, for example, may have an IT mix-up which it has to untangle. In addition to following this storyline, you can add comedic elements to any kind of story to make it more fun for the audience. Humor is a great emotion to trigger and it makes your story more memorable.

Tragedy

In a tragedy, the hero has some fatal character flaw, weakness or has a lapse in judgment, and it gradually leads to their undoing. We, as an audience, feel empathy, or pity for the tragic hero, like Shakespeare's *Macbeth*, because he is haunted and tormented by his unfortunate circumstance, nearly always succumbing to it in the end.

Examples of tragedies include *Bonnie and Clyde*, John Steinbeck's *Of Mice and Men*, *Westside Story*, and *Titanic*.

Tragedy stories are the toughest to use in marketing. But I've listed it here so you'd know it when you saw it.

Rebirth

Finally, the rebirth story is one that can be used very effectively in marketing. This is a story in which someone sinks to their lowest, most hopeless point, and then makes a miraculous recovery. The struggle of the main character offers a conflict to the story, and overcoming the struggle and rising from the ashes is inspirational to the audience.

In *A Christmas Carol*, Scrooge threatens to stop Christmas, but the holiday is saved in the end. There's an element of rebirth in nearly every season of *Doctor Who*. *Beauty and the Beast* and *Despicable Me* are both rebirth stories.

There are a great number of rebirth story ideas in a business context. Your product could save people right at the moment when they're at the very bottom. This plot can also be worked into customer testimonials. Your brand story could be about your business facing hardship and near bankruptcy until a great idea saves the day. Any personal story about overcoming a hardship or dark time is a rebirth story.

The rebirth story you tell doesn't even have to do with your company, but can focus on the theme your brand represents. An excellent example is Gatorade's "Replay" series, which told the story of two ice hockey teams who took to the ice eleven years after a game which had involved a near fatal accident for one player. The story isn't really about Gatorade at all. Gatorade only sponsors the game and you just see their products peripherally in the footage.

As you've undoubtedly noticed from the above examples, an individual story can have multiple storylines within it. A hero may go on a journey to conquer a monster, only to face a serious and near-fatal struggle from which he/she experiences a rebirth, and then return home at the end. You don't have to restrict yourself to only one storyline. Most great stories combine traces of a few.

The combination is up to you. However, no matter which plot you use, there are a few elements that you must include. Let's take a look at those.

Story Elements

In addition to the plot points outlined earlier, your story (every story, really) should have the following elements to keep it engaging and memorable.

Emotional Connection

Earlier, we talked about how stories trigger parts of our brain related to emotion. The more the characters of your story experience emotions common to the audience, the closer they will identify with the character. In turn, they will feel more connected to the story. It will stick with them and remain more memorable.

Relatable Characters

Stories have little effect if we don't relate to their characters. Being able to see themselves in a character or their actions is one of the critical elements of keeping an audience engaged with the story. Showing the vulnerable or flawed side of your characters gives the audience more opportunities to relate to them.

When asked why someone is ambivalent about a story, one of the first criticisms you'll hear is, "I couldn't relate." Just think back to any TV show you watched or book you read where you didn't really care whether the characters lived or died. It wasn't very compelling, was it?

When we can relate to the characters in your story, it keeps us engaged. We're rooting for the heroine and hoping that she'll win. We hope the hero returns home, conquers the monster, bounces back from their huge setback, or reaches the goal at journey's end.

Suspense and Tension

Suspense and tension are important elements in any story. They keep the audience glued to the story to see what will happen in the end. Although everybody knows that James Bond won't get killed by the villain an hour into the movie, we're still on the edge of our seats as we watch the drill get closer to his head. Interestingly, suspense and tension are more powerful in storytelling than the rational mind, which, given the time to think it through, would say, "That would never happen."

Inspiration

Stories don't have to be inspirational to be interesting (remember the tragedy storyline). But when it comes to telling stories in a marketing context, you generally want to inspire your audience. A fundraising ad that shows starving children isn't meant to drive you to despair and give up hope. They always deliver the message that you can make a difference.

Inspiration is important because it influences the person to take action. Taking action could mean buying a product or making a donation. But it could be something more subtle such as allying yourself with a brand and its vision. Stories that don't offer this hope and inspiration don't lead the audience to take action.

In this chapter we learned how to structure a good story, and looked the basic plots we could apply, as well as the core elements that must be included. In the next chapter, we are going to put it into practice.

DON'T SELL ME, TELL ME

Finding Your Theme

What do you stand for?

In the last chapter we looked at the different categories of stories and how they might work for a business, along with the core elements that must to be in your story. Now it's time to start applying the elements to create your story.

But where do you start?

One good way of narrowing down all the possibilities is to begin with the end in mind. That is to say, let's find the core theme — the moral of the story, if you will.

The best way to do that is to get total clarity of purpose for you and your company. We learned earlier how - as a business owner - your personal story is closely tied with your brand. So by achieving clarity about why you do what you do, what you stand for and who can benefit most from your skills and passion, you'll have an easier time staying congruent with your brand story.

Without clarity, creating a story that is aligned with your values is a complete shot in the dark.

This is important work. It's not just a theoretical exercise. Take the time to do it and you'll be amazed at how much stronger your brand can be. But like anytime when we have to look in the mirror and potentially expose to ourselves that we've been behaving out of character, it may be a bit uncomfortable. Your tendency may be to skip over it. Please don't. Uncovering and defining your purpose is the bedrock, the foundation of building a story that connects with your audience.

Remember, honest emotions are the strongest.

Resist, also, the inclination to say, "My business is not that different," "I'm not that unique," or "My story is boring." You must push through those urges, because they are simply a smokescreen; lies that we've been telling ourselves instead of actually opening up to ourselves. As you'll soon see, your business is unique, because you are unique.

To get you started, here are some exercises to help you define your core values and purpose.

1. Brainstorm as many ideas as you can about why you do what you do. What motivates you to get out of bed every morning? Is it the kudos and acknowledgment of work well done? Is it getting awards and being respected by your peers? Is it serving the community? Helping others in need? Seeing others succeed? List as many ideas as you can, apart from money.

2. List everything at which you are skillful, regardless of whether or not you enjoy it or

if you think it is valuable to your business in any way. Just write down as many things as you can that you are good at as they come into your head. What do people naturally ask you about, in and out of work? You don't need to be the best in the world. Keep writing until you fill the paper with all of your skills.

3. Next, write down everything you enjoy about your business. Answer this question honestly and don't fool yourself. If you hate some task, whether the business requires it or not, don't write it down. If you love some other aspect - even if you don't currently make any money from it - still write it down. Just fill a page with everything you love doing in your business.

4. Look for patterns and themes. Identify any crossover between your skills and your passion to find your sweet spot. For example, are you a natural connector? Are you a detail person, finding joy in the finesse? Ideally, you should keep writing

until you find between five and ten things that flow in a similar vein and contribute to making up your sweet spot.

5. Now it's time to articulate your theme. State it in terms of what you stand for. It's okay to be bold. What is it, when someone works with you, they are guaranteed to get? What do you always deliver, what do you believe in, and would never give up? What is "your promise" to the world?

It's valuable to state, also, what you stand against. What gets you angry about your industry or your business? When people interact with you, what is it that they will never get? Write these down. We are starting to get to the core of what you value most. This is what your customers are craving too.

The theme, or moral of all the stories you tell should align with your values. The more honest you are, the stronger the theme. The stronger the theme, the more powerful your brand.

QUICK NOTE:

We've assembled some worksheets and tools to help you with these exercises. Go to http://dontsellmetellmebook.com/member/ to download them for free.

Now, there are many, many ways to communicate your theme. In the next chapter, we are going to look at how to set the tone for your stories — your brand voice. But how do you find your voice?

Character Archetypes

Some people have jovial personalities, some people are more serious. You look to some people for their knowledge, some for their ability to relate. Likewise, your brand and therefore your stories, will have a personality, or "voice." Ideally, as we've talked about, it will be close to your voice.

A great way to help guide your team on what voice to use when telling a story for and about your business is to give it a "character." Characters in stories generally fall into a set of archetypes. Not coincidently, so do people.

The term "archetype" has its origins in ancient Greek. The root words are *archein*, which means "original or old"; and *typos*, which means "pattern, model or type." The combined meaning is an "original pattern" of which all other similar persons, objects, or concepts are derived, copied, modeled, or emulated.

Carl Jung, the psychologist, used the concept of archetype in his theories of the human psyche. Based on the ideas of Plato, he believed that universal character types reside within the collective unconscious of people all over the world. Archetypes represent the fundamental human motifs we experienced as we evolved, and therefore, they connect deeply to our emotions.

Jung defined twelve primary archetypes that symbolize our basic human motivations. Each type has its own set of values, goals and personality traits. Also, the twelve types can be grouped into three sets of four each: Ego, Soul and Self. The types in each set share a common driving source. The archetypes within the Ego set are driven to fulfill ego-defined agendas. The archetypes within the Soul set are driven to fulfill soul-satisfying agendas. And the archetypes within the Self set are driven to fulfill agendas defined by self.

These three labels are not judgments, just a way of grouping common motivations. The Self types are not selfish, the Ego types are not egotists. One is not better than the other.

Most, if not all, people have several archetypes at play at the same time. However, you'll find one archetype tends to be predominant. It can be helpful to know which archetypes you most identify with, because it will give you personal insight into your motivations and values.

Read through the following major archetypes and see if you can identify the dominant one in your personality. If you are honest with yourself, when you are reading the underlying desires, goals and strengths, one will start to ring true. You may find it's a great starting point, shedding light on what voice to use for your business.

THE EGO TYPES

1. The Innocent
Motto: Free to be you and me
Core Desire: to get to paradise
Goal: to be happy
Strategy: to do the right thing
Talent: faith and optimism
Weakness: boring for all their naive innocence
Greatest Fear: to be punished for doing something bad or wrong

The Innocent is also known as: The Romantic, Utopian, Traditionalist, Naive

2. The Orphan/The Everyman
Motto: All men and women are created equal
Core Desire: connecting with others
Goal: to belong

Strategy: develop ordinary solid virtues, be down to earth, the common touch

Talent: realism, empathy, lack of pretense

Weakness: losing one's own self in an effort to blend in or for the sake of superficial relationships

Greatest Fear: to be left out or to stand out from the crowd

The Everyman is also known as: The Regular Guy or Gal, Person Next Door, Realist, Solid Citizen, Good Neighbor

3. The Hero

Motto: Where there's a will, there's a way

Core Desire: to prove one's worth through courageous acts

Goal: mastery in a way that improves the world

Strategy: to be as strong and competent as possible

Talent: competence and courage

Weakness: arrogance, always needing another battle to fight

Greatest Fear: weakness, vulnerability, being a "chicken"

The Hero is also known as: The Warrior, Crusader, Rescuer, Soldier, Dragon Slayer

4. The Caregiver
Motto: Love your neighbor as yourself
Core Desire: to protect and care for others
Goal: to help others
Strategy: doing things for others
Talent: compassion, generosity
Weakness: martyrdom and being exploited
Greatest Fear: selfishness and ingratitude

The Caregiver is also known as: The Saint, Altruist, Parent, Helper, Supporter

THE SOUL TYPES

5. The Explorer
Motto: Don't fence me in
Core Desire: the freedom to find out who you are through exploring the world
Goal: to experience a better, more authentic, more fulfilling life

Strategy: journey, seeking out and experiencing new things, escape from boredom

Talent: autonomy, ambition, being true to one's soul

Weakness: aimless wandering, becoming a misfit

Greatest Fear: getting trapped, conformity, and inner emptiness

The Explorer is also known as: The Seeker, Wanderer, Individualist, Pilgrim

6. The Rebel

Motto: Rules are made to be broken

Core Desire: revenge or revolution

Goal: to overturn what isn't working

Strategy: disrupt, destroy, or shock

Talent: outrageousness, radical freedom

Weakness: crossing over to the dark side, crime

Greatest Fear: to be powerless or ineffectual

The Rebel is also known as: The Outlaw, Revolutionary, Wild One, Misfit

7. The Lover

Motto: You're the only one

Core Desire: intimacy and experience

Goal: being in a relationship with the people, work and surroundings they love

Strategy: to become more and more physically and emotionally attractive

Talent: passion, gratitude, appreciation, and commitment

Weakness: outward-directed desire to please others at risk of losing own identity

Greatest Fear: being alone, a wallflower, unwanted, unloved

The Lover is also known as: The Partner, Friend, Intimate, Enthusiast, Sensualist

8. The Creator

Motto: If you can imagine it, it can be done

Core Desire: to create things of enduring value

Goal: to realize a vision

Strategy: develop artistic control and skill

Talent: creativity and imagination

Weakness: perfectionism, unfinished projects

Greatest Fear: mediocre vision or execution

The Creator is also known as: The Artist, Inventor, Innovator, Craftsman, Musician, Writer, Dreamer

THE SELF TYPES

9. The Jester
Motto: You only live once
Core Desire: to live in the moment with full enjoyment
Goal: to have a great time and lighten up the world
Strategy: play, make jokes, be funny
Talent: joy
Weakness: frivolity, wasting time
Greatest Fear: being bored or boring others

The Jester is also known as: The Fool, Trickster, Joker, Comedian

10. The Sage
Motto: The truth will set you free
Core Desire: to find the truth
Goal: to use intelligence and analysis to understand the world

Strategy: seeking out information and knowledge; self-reflection and understanding thought processes
Talent: wisdom, intelligence
Weakness: can study details forever and never act
Greatest Fear: being duped, misled, or ignorance

The Sage is also known as: The Scholar, Detective, Philosopher, Researcher, Mentor

11. The Magician

Motto: I make things happen
Core Desire: understanding the fundamental laws of the universe
Goal: to make dreams come true
Strategy: develop a vision and live by it
Talent: finding win-win solutions
Weakness: becoming manipulative
Greatest Fear: unintended negative consequences

The Magician is also known as: The Visionary, Catalyst, Shaman, Healer, Medicine Man

12. The Ruler

Motto: Power isn't everything, it's the only thing

Core Desire: control

Goal: create a prosperous, successful family or community

Strategy: exercise power

Talent: responsibility, leadership

Weakness: being authoritarian, unable to delegate

Greatest Fear: chaos, being overthrown

The Ruler is also known as: The Boss, Leader, Aristocrat, King, Queen, Politician

Which of these archetypes most reflects what you value? Can you see how the basic desires and fears, goals and talents align with your core values and purpose? These exercises will give you a good starting point to developing your brand voice. But there are two sides to any conversation, so let's look at the other side, your target audience.

Finding the Audience

"If a story is not about the hearer he [or she] will not listen. . . A great lasting story is about everyone or it will not last. The strange and foreign is not interesting - only the deeply personal and familiar."

— John Steinbeck, *East of Eden*

By now, you probably have some ideas swarming in your head about stories you can use for your brand, company, products, or customers. You've discovered your theme and the voice you'll use to convey it. The next step is to consider your audience.

When it comes to storytelling, it's not the story itself that determines its effectiveness. It needs to resonate with and connect with your audience. To make the strongest connection, you need to know your audience as well as you can. You need to understand them better than they understand themselves. So, who, specifically, is your ideal audience?

The key word here is specifically.

Of course, you need to understand your market's demographics, such as age, gender, economic level and perhaps location. But don't stop there. More important, you need to understand what they value most, what they desire, and what keeps them up at night. The fancy word for this is psychographics. Psychographics help you get to the thoughts, feelings, opinions and values that drive attitudes. If your story is in sync with the attitudes and values of your audience, it will feel familiar and you'll connect on an emotional level.

So, be as specific as you can.

A 33 year old single mother, trying to make ends meet has different needs and motivation from a 55 year old man, trapped in an 80 hour a week job, struggling to make time for his kids.

The more specifically you can describe your audience, the more you can reflect their feelings and emotions in your stories. When the listener sees his or her feelings and circumstances reflected back at them, it's very powerful. That kind of story sticks with them. The theme is felt deeper and it has the power to move them to action.

So, be as specific as you can.

If you are having trouble nailing down your ideal audience, don't despair. It's more common in business than you think. When I consult with clients, there seems to be a natural resistance to narrowing down their target audience. Why would you "turn away" business? So, this brings us to an important distinction. There is a difference between "marketing to" and "selling to." And different decisions to be made within each activity. Identifying your ideal audience doesn't necessarily mean you won't take someone outside that group as a customer (although it could).

Identifying and talking to a specific audience opens the possibility of creating a deeper emotional connection with them. And it's only through that kind of connection that you turn transactional customers into loyal fans. That won't happen when you are speaking generally, to a broad group. Trying to make everyone happy won't really make anyone happy.

Imagine this example: if you owned a women's shoe store that sold only expensive, high-heeled pumps, you'd naturally speak only to fashionable women with your story. If a man came in to buy a pair, however, you'd still sell it to him, wouldn't you? But now imagine how much less effective your marketing messages would be if every advertisement had to include fashionable women — PLUS any man, just in case... Changes the way your ideal audience (the fashionable women) would feel about your brand, wouldn't it?

There will be times when it doesn't make business sense to sell to anyone outside your ideal audience. If it affects profitability, for instance. The point here is that the decisions about marketing and sales are related, but they are separate decisions.

That should take a little pressure off being okay with narrowing down your ideal audience and getting specific in describing them. If you are still having some difficulty, here's another way of looking at it:

Imagine we were working together and I were able to get you ten or even a hundred more clients, but they all had to be duplicates or clones of one of your current customers. Which one would it be? Write it down.

Start there and describe everything you can about that one customer. Use their name, even. What, specifically (there's that word again) does he or she value most? What do they fear most? What words do they use to describe working with you? How do they feel when working with you?

This is as good a place as any to start.

In the next section, you'll see how those same emotions can be used to make your story strong.

Finding the Emotion

Remember how Emotion is one of the elements every story must have to keep its audience engaged? As soon as you get a clear picture of the specific goals and desires of your ideal audience, you can make conscious decisions about the key emotions you'll be going for in your story. Start with the list of fears and feelings you just wrote down (you did do the exercise, didn't you?), so you can connect with your audience's pain points, values and desires.

With consistency, your customers will remain connected through those emotions when they consume your content, buy your products and otherwise interact with your brand. This is, in fact, what builds a strong memorable brand.

There are as many ways to combine plot, characters, themes and emotions as there are people on this planet. That's why, using story, you can create a unique position in your market, even when you occupy the same niche, in the same industry, as another company.

For example, a change in emotion may be all it takes. A family restaurant is going to appeal to different emotions in its stories than a law firm or a software security company, even if it shares the same basic plot. A law firm may create a cautionary tale, while a security firm appeals to fear in its stories. The software security company's story may involve a hero (you) conquering a monster (a hacking attack) using a special weapon (its software). A family restaurant may tell the story of a group of heroes (your family) conquering a different monster (the stress of daily life) by taking the kids out to enjoy good food and a good time.

Nonprofit organizations often use compassion as the emotion in their stories. When you see the child in need gazing out at you from a photograph, you would be hard-pressed not to feel compassion, which is the driver for people likely to donate to a nonprofit organization.

In the last section, we wrote down the words your ideal audience uses to describe working with you.

Or how they feel when working with you. Another good question to ask is: how did they feel BEFORE they worked with you? Or what would they be experiencing if they never found you?

These are the questions that will get you close to the emotions you want to have in your stories.

Next we are going to look at the easiest way to use them to their greatest advantage, and how not to trip yourself up while doing so.

Telling Your Story

Build on Your Theme

Most companies when they start to develop a brand think about their logo or their business cards or maybe their website. But as we've seen, your brand is actually tied closely to your values. And by nurturing your values, you develop a theme. And out of your theme grows your story.

Decisions come easier after that. Once you start to fill in the structure of your story, then it's a matter of choosing how to express it.

So structure your story first, then create or design all the materials that help tell the story. Do it the other way around and most likely you'll be making decisions that are not in support of your story and you'll eventually get in your own way! So avoid the wasted time and expense and pay attention to the story first.

Start with your values, then your theme, character archetype and emotional tone. Once you've got the elements of your story in place, your entire marketing and advertising platform can grow out of it.

You are most likely not going to execute all of your marketing alone, so your story and your theme make it easier for your designer, your writers, and everyone on your team to work towards the same goal. And for you to make decisions or to approve the work they do. "Does it serve the story?" is the deciding factor, removing most of the arbitrary opinions.

Having your story nailed helps determine the tone of the copywriting, informs how the logo should look, what colors to use, what to focus on when building your website. All in service of the story.

When developing your story, it's important to remember that honesty is endearing, and people don't see jargon as honest. They see it as mumbo-jumbo, subconsciously registering that something is being covered up. So try to stay grounded. Authentic emotions will always connect better than spin.

And don't try too hard. Think about the person who announces before telling a joke that, "I've got a funny joke!" Instantly, everyone else within earshot is saying to themselves, "I'll be the judge of that." It puts you in a position of fighting an uphill battle. Just by saying its funny already lessens the chances that it will be.

The same, by the way, goes for creativity. Declaring you are creative is the kiss of death. Exercise humility. The proof should be in the pudding.

So there's no need to try too hard. Focus on staying true to your values. If you haven't done so yet, go back through the last chapters and do the exercises so you have those values in mind as we take the next steps.

Over time, if each story you tell supports the overall theme, they in essence become part of a much bigger story. The concept or idea behind your brand shines through. For example, each small story of Apple's design innovation adds to the strength of Apple's legendary design philosophy. Likewise, each story of how you helped someone's life, or solved someone's problem adds to the bigger purpose of your company's mission.

They say actions define a person's character. Well, the same holds true for your brand. Each thing you do should be part of something bigger.

There's a simple way to stay on course as you build on your theme. We'll look at that next.

Stay True

Robert McKee, an internationally-respected seminar leader, screenplay consultant and author of the seminal book, *Story: Style, Structure, Substance, and the Principles of Screenwriting*, reminds writers that, "story unearths a universally human experience, then wraps itself inside a unique, culture-specific expression."

As we develop stories for our business, it's important to keep reminding ourselves that the best stories are authentic and immediately ring true for the listener. This is why often you can find great stories by simply looking around you and keeping your eyes and ears open. Look at your past history, or your company's history. Tell stories about real events, real people and real situations. Anything that happens which you find interesting could be elaborated and turned into a story that your audience would also connect with.

In filmmaking, even science fiction, the successful stories tackle topics common to each of us. Only the 'world' in which the stories take place is different. The 'truth' is in how the character felt, not in the surroundings. The television series *Star Trek* was successful, not because of the special effects, but because it appealed to ethical, emotional and human struggles that we all have.

Another idea, which helps root your stories in reality, is to get your customers to create your stories for you. Customer-generated content is great not only because it's authentic but also because you can be fairly certain it's on target. If one customer struggled with or overcame an issue, you can bet there are more customers just like them. This approach is also a huge timesaver! It's a shortcut to finding great stories because you don't need to start from scratch. All you need to do is structure it and elaborate.

Keeping the stories real also serves as a guide, making it easier to see when they veer too far from supporting your theme.

Collecting customer stories isn't difficult. You can simply listen to your customers and identify good stories as they tell them, or send a survey or put out a call to your audience and have them submit their stories.

Using your customers' experiences is not only a way to stay on target; it also helps avoid another common trap with beginning storytellers, which we are going to examine next.

The I in Story

You've probably heard the old maxim, "There is no 'I' in Team." Well, the less 'I' in your story, the better. In the best marketing stories, the product (you) is in the background. When telling a story, focus on making it a good story, not on promoting the brand or product. Just like other forms of content marketing, your story will do the selling for you.

If you're telling a product story, of course the product will tend to take center stage. Its benefits will be a major part of the story. But remember that it doesn't have to be, and in general, the less promoting the better. In many good story ads, the product or brand isn't even mentioned.

The best stories reflect the benefits of the product without actually saying it. The viewer will make that connection in their mind, and the connection is much stronger when they do it on their own.

When considering the characters for your story, use people who reflect the values of your market. Choose characters your audience can identify with, the people who will make them say, "That guy is just like me," or "I know someone just like that gal." Whenever possible, use real customers and real employees.

Besides reflecting your ideal audience in your stories, there is another tool you have at your disposal that will make your stories instantly engaging, so let's talk about that next.

Visual Language

A picture, and by extension a video, says a thousand words. This is no exaggeration. The more visual elements you add into your story, the deeper the meaning, the more it "speaks" to the audience. In fact, you can create images that tell stories without any words at all. The reason visual elements make stories more effective is that they more directly trigger emotions.

You don't necessarily need images to trigger a visual response. Use visual language as much as possible. How do you do that? With detail. The more specifics you can include in your descriptions, the more visual it becomes. When writing your story, don't try to sound lofty and "literate." Write using a simple, personal tone that's easy for your audience to understand and relate to. If you're not much of a writer yourself, you can easily hire a writer to craft your story from your outline.

Images, however, carry an additional benefit. In social media, the more interesting imagery you use, the more likely it will be shared.

But for now, try to be as detailed as possible when describing people and situations, and paint a picture with your words.

Some business owners find this a difficult adjustment because storytelling is not a skill they've developed, yet. If you need help, you can always work with people who are experts in the skills that you lack. The good news is, it's possible to outsource every step of this process.

But when we work with clients — even when we are creating one hundred percent of the content for you — we encourage you to be an active participant in developing the theme and character voice. It's your story, so it should sound like you!

You now have the basic building blocks for developing your story: your purpose and values, your voice, the ideal audience and their desires. We looked at where to start for story ideas and how to use these ideas to continually build a strong brand. In the next chapter we'll look at a few places you can immediately start using your story.

Where and When

Where to Tell Your Story

Now that you have a theme, a voice and some story ideas, you'll need to decide where you'll tell your story. There are a multitude of places to tell your story and as many types of media to use. Overall, keep in mind that the most important factor for where to tell your story and what form it should take is where ever your target market is.

What kind of media does your ideal audience consume? Some people like reading text content while others don't. Certain demographics prefer images or video. You'll need to look at the content your market already consumes and then adapt your presentation to that.

To start, we're going to look at a few places that are ideal for trying out your new-found storytelling skills.

Your About Page

A great place to begin telling your story is on your website. Your website is not chiseled in stone, so it's an ideal platform to test out your story.

Many companies include their company story as part of their website's About page. In most cases, the About page is the second most visited page on your website after the Home page. But if your website is like most websites, the About page currently reads like a resume. That's such a waste, because there is little value in that. You are making the visitor do all the work of seeing if you are someone they want to learn more about.

Here's a secret: your About page should really be about them!

So take a look at your About page and apply the elements of story. Start by describing the "before" world you or your customers experienced, and if your description is vivid, you'll have them hooked right from the beginning. Then take them on a short journey. Whether it's a rags to riches story, a voyage and return, or a comedy, your visitor will be more likely to remember you, your core values and what you offer. They'll also begin to know what it feels like to work with you - and that does more of a job selling faster than any list of capabilities or past achievements.

HERE'S A BONUS TIP:
Once your About page story is written, I encourage you to turn it into a video. It doesn't have to be long - a short video of you telling your story instantly allows more of a connection to be made. Your audience gets not only a feel for what working with you is like, but they also leave feeling that they "know you" a little bit more.

That familiarity will pay off when they are in the buying phase of the sales cycle.

Your Blog

Personal stories and customer stories make great blog content. Blogging, really, has always been about telling personal stories. That's what the medium was invented for. Blogs started as "web logs," or an online journal. If you create blog articles using personal stories, the key to making them work for you is to add "takeaways" to the story, or tips or insights drawn from the story that can immediately help the reader.

Your blog is also a great environment to test parts of your story. Each blog can be a segment of the overall "plot." This gives your audience the feeling of making the journey with you. A shared journey can forge a powerful relationship.

That perceived rapport will pay off big time. Your audience, by reading your series of blog articles, on the same theme over time, will see you as an expert in your topic. This builds trust, and you haven't done any selling. When they are in the buying stage, your ideal prospect will go with the person they trust.

ANOTHER BONUS TIP:
On your blog, even when writing in a visual style, it's always good to include images and visuals. Blog posts are generally scanned, and the images will keep your reader engaged when scrolling down the page. And as we discussed earlier, if your blog post gets shared, a shared post with an image will get more clicks than one without.

Networking

Telling your stories in person is another great place to practice telling your stories. You've probably heard of creating an elevator pitch for networking events. An elevator pitch is a short statement about how you position your business, often used as an opener at networking events. It's called an elevator pitch to get you to imagine a scenario where you only have a short time to get all the important information stated — as if you stepped on an elevator with an important potential client, and you had to give your pitch to her before the elevator reached it's destination.

(Although I've been in some pretty slow elevators, but I'm sure you get the point.)

The purpose of the elevator pitch is to succinctly tell the listener all about what you do and how you can help them. What an elevator pitch is not designed to do is entertain, or determine if the listener is even interested in the first place.

Leading with an elevator pitch is dangerous, because not only is there a distinct risk you'll come off as sales-y; if the other party is not interested, the conversation dies right there.

So here's another approach: at the next networking event, try listening first. Then, armed with the elements of story, offer an appropriate story from one of the story types we discussed earlier. Maybe a customer story about how they overcame a similar problem. If the story connects with the other person, and triggers a positive emotion, they will let you know they are interested in hearing more.

That's when you can use the elevator pitch. When they've actually asked for it.

Entertain and enlighten someone, and they will most likely ask for more. And if on the rare occasion they aren't interested, then at the very least they walk away with the impression that you are someone who adds value to a conversation, not just a sales person.

Your Emails

If you're doing email marketing, make storytelling an integral part of the emails you send your subscribers. This will boost your clickthrough rates as well as help to solidify your brand image. Even if you are not running email marketing campaigns, any time you create and distribute a story on another channel, like your blog, be sure to let your email list know about it too.

There is an all-too-common acronym/expression regarding emails: TL;DR. It means "Too Long, Didn't Read." Emails should be very short: some experts preach no more than five sentences. I happen to agree with that. So you'll only be able to tell short stories, or in most cases, a part of the story that gives flavor or context to the email. Use little vignettes or snippets of a larger story.

If you are sending an email newsletter, use the short story or beginning snippet as a teaser to click through to read the full blog post. Remember to keep your theme and brand voice in mind, so the emails don't wander. You want each customer touch point to support the greater whole.

You now have a few excellent places to start practicing your new storytelling skills. Pick one, and start today. Then as you get comfortable, you'll start to see new places to introduce story into your business communications. It won't stop there. Storytelling is a continuing practice.

In the next chapter, we'll talk about some ways to manage that ongoing journey.

Your Evolving Story

Story Within a Story

Once you've done the work to find your theme and discover your character archetype and voice, you don't have to map your story out perfectly before telling any of it. Choose the plot that most suits you as of today. Over time, you may find you need multiple stories to describe various aspects of your business.

Your story will naturally evolve over time. It has to: since you cannot predict the future, there are some parts of your story that are as yet unwritten!

Consider this just the first installment. You may have one installment for how you founded the business, and one for the growth phase. Installments can be chronological but they don't have to be.

Installments can simply be related stories within a bigger story. A classic example in literature is *One Thousand and One Nights*, commonly called *Arabian Nights*. Told by the character Scheherazade, each story is a tale that ties in to the entire collection. This is what you're doing when you create a number of short stories that all follow a similar theme or topic.

Another effective storytelling technique is to break up the story into chapters. Chapters don't have to stand completely on their own. Like scenes from a movie, chapters will have a beginning, middle and end, but the end of a chapter usually sets the reader up to want to continue reading the next chapter. This is a good way to keep your audience tuned in for the next installment.

As you improve, more and more of your audience will not only stay tuned for the next "chapter," but will actually start anticipating your next communication. When that happens, your potential audience begins to transform from casual readers into a tribe of loyal fans that know, like and trust you. They'll listen to your recommendations and even share them. And when your fans are recommending you — of their own volition — you are in a position to profit like never before.

Let's take a quick look at how to make that happen faster.

Share Worthy

As you start to tell your stories, pay attention to the reaction. Some parts will be well received, some parts not as much. Some parts will resonate better than others. And some, will actually get shared.

When your story gets shared, that's better than free advertising. Better, because unlike paid advertising, a shared story is more personal. It's more like a personal recommendation, so it carries more weight.

How can you get more of your story shared?

Have you ever been at a cocktail party — or any gathering, for that matter — and shared a story you heard earlier on the radio or shared a story about what happened to you when you were on your way somewhere earlier in the day? How did you feel? Why do you think you shared the story?

If you are like most people, you share a story because you think it will enlighten or entertain your listener. It makes us feel good, and reflects well on us, when we feel we've helped another person, that they got "value" from us in some way.

Now, have you ever been at a party, maybe even the same party, and overheard someone sharing a story they heard, and it was the same story you told just before? They were sharing your story! How do you think they were feeling? What made them share a story that wasn't even theirs? Probably for the same reason you told it in the first place - to enlighten or entertain their listener. They were probably feeling good that they were adding "value" to their conversation. It's a good reflection on them and they were, in a way, proud to be associated with the story.

Having something reflect well on you, having that feeling of pride, that's a pretty strong emotion to tap into.

All of the content that gets widely shared has one thing in common – it sparks strong emotions. They trigger a closely held value in the audience and because that value is important to them, they want others to know it. These stories are awe-inspiring, amusing, moving, illuminating, inspiring, shocking, cute, sexy, scary, infuriating or controversial.

Of course, you want to make sure the tone is appropriate for your brand and audience. But pay attention to the emotions your stories are triggering, and which ones get the stronger reactions. They will help your stories get shared.

Now let's talk about what to do when they don't get shared.

Revise

"A story is based on what people think is important, so when we live a story, we are telling people around us what we think is important."

— Donald Miller, *A Million Miles in a Thousand Years: What I Learned While Editing My Life*

Few people will get their story perfectly the first time they try. But this is not a failure. Use the feedback from your audience to constantly refine your story or stories until they have the desired impact.

Even if your first few tries are not as perfect as you'd like, you'll get better and better at storytelling the more you do it. As long as you stay true to your values, your purpose and your theme, you'll be heading in the right direction. Keep what works, revise the rest.

And don't stop. Just by practicing, you will improve.

As you and your business grow, circumstances will change. You'll have more events that may contribute to your plot. You'll always need to adjust the way you tell your stories. Remember, there will be many ways to express the same theme, so don't feel any one story is set in stone.

Big brands have been telling their stories for a long time and are constantly evolving. We don't notice the evolution as much because it happens over the course of years or decades. You may fear you are making too many changes to your stories, but you will have a heightened awareness the rest of your audience doesn't have. The reality is the rest of the world is not paying that close attention. The good news is, they'll be far more accepting and see it as variations on a theme.

So don't be afraid of evolving. In fact expect you will have to.

To be continued...

I've given you a lot to process in this book. Your head is probably swirling with ideas and possible uses for stories in your business. You may also be thinking this is a lot to take in and worried about "doing it right."

Let's do a quick recap, and then discuss the keys for quickly implementing this in your business. We talked about why stories are so engaging, and how they are the only way for you to stop spinning the same jargon that sounds like most every other business out there. We looked at how being honest with ourselves creates a more authentic, and therefore stronger foundation for your stories.

I showed you the secret link between your values and your brand, and how it forms unbeatable connections with your ideal audience. From there we looked at how to use multiple types of stories to connect with your specific target. Then we broke down the structure, basic plots and elements of a good story. Then we explored how to effectively apply the elements to you and your business to find your theme and character voice. And finally, we talked about how and where to begin telling your stories.

Yeah, I guess it is a lot to take in all at once. If any of this is new to you, you might feel overwhelmed, leaving you wondering what to do next. And if you are more familiar with the structure of story, you may be tempted to gloss over all this advice - and still do nothing. I urge you, in both scenarios, to re-read each section, and this time, after each section, write down some ideas for how the concepts might apply to you.

Then, if you are still feeling stuck, know that you don't have to do it alone.

You probably assumed that my company offers further training and assistance to help individuals and business owners to implement compelling stories in their business. You assumed correctly.

We've helped organizations large and small, from freelancers to nonprofit organizations, from creative artists to accountants. And they all benefitted by using these storytelling techniques.

Go to http://dontsellmetellmebook.com/profit/ to see a detailed case study on how we helped one of our clients increase traffic, leads and sales.

So, What's Your Story?

If you want to rebuild trust and connect with your audience in a meaningful, lasting way, you need to stop saying the same things everyone else is saying. Stop sounding like everyone else and tell your own, unique story.

As soon as you do, the right people will respond. Not everyone will respond, and that's okay. In fact, it's desirable. Because the connections you make will be stronger, and more beneficial to you and your business.

Imagine what it will be like to build a group of people who are actually interested in what you have to say, and cannot wait to hear what you have to say next. It's easier, more profitable and more rewarding when you are working with the people you were meant to serve.

Crafting your unique story is not complicated, but it takes some effort. Only a small percentage of people who read this book will actually take some action on these ideas, and apply it to their business.

I want you to be one of the few that decides now is the time to tell your own story.

People are waiting to hear what you have to say. I'm one of them.

You are about to change your business forever. You are about to rewrite the story of your business. It's up to you what goes into your next chapter.

Resources

When you're ready to start using storytelling to build a base of strong, loyal fans, we've assembled some worksheets and tools to help you.

Make sure to go to http://dontsellmetellmebook.com/member/ to get all the extra training and resources that go along with this book.

Please and Thank You

Thank you for purchasing and reading *Don't Sell Me, Tell Me*. As a business owner, I know your time is precious, and you could have picked from a lot of books. Including Facebook. Or a million other things that are pulling at your attention.

But you chose to spend your time with me. So THANK YOU.

If you considered leaving an honest review on Amazon so I can provide even better solutions for you, then I want you to know that the thought does count. So THANK YOU for that, too.

If you actually left a review on Amazon, then, jeepers! That requires the biggest thank you of all. So assume I am looking directly at you, (because I would be, if we were in the same room) when I say, most sincerely,

Thank you, thank, you, THANK YOU!

In case you haven't got the hint, yet: Please leave an honest review on Amazon. It helps independent authors like me, a lot!

SELF-PUBLISHING
SCHOOL

Now It's Your Turn

Ever Dream of Turning Your Story Into a Book?

If you know me at all, you know I'm a bit of a perfectionist. What that means is, it takes me forever to start a project, and no one will ever call me "speedy" during the creation process. But investing in Self-Publishing School helped me get from zero book idea to published in just three months!

Pretty cool.

Even cooler, they explain the EXACT 3-step blueprint in a FREE VIDEO SERIES!

Go to http://dontsellmetellmebook.com/sps to watch them.

So even if you're busy, bad at writing, or don't know where to start, you can write a bestseller and build your best life.

With tools and experience across a variety niches and professions, Self-Publishing School really is the only resource you need to take your book to the finish line.

SO, STOP DREAMING AND START WRITING

Watch this free video series now, and say "Yes" to becoming a bestselling author.

Here is the link again to the videos:
http://dontsellmetellmebook.com/sps

(Seriously, what are you waiting for?)

Acknowledgements

I wish to say thank you to the following for their invaluable contributions to this book:

To my wife Terry, whose mission to bring more veracity to business and in life inspired the premise.

To Doug Barry and Scott Allan, for keeping me accountable.

To Chandler Bolt and the team at Self-Publishing School, who really do have it down.

DON'T SELL ME, TELL ME

About Greg Koorhan

Greg Koorhan is an award-winning filmmaker and co-founder of Crossbow Studio (CrossbowStudio.com), an independent film and video production company specializing in uplifting stories that inspire, educate and entertain. He is also the founder of ProfitArcher (ProfitArcher.com); a digital marketing firm focused on helping you generate leads for your business by creating compelling content aimed straight at the heart of your audience.

He lives just outside of Philadelphia with his wife, Terry. And even though their two children are out of the house, he feels blessed they are both pursuing their passions with abandon, and creating their own stories.

You can send Greg an email and say "Hey" at: gkoorhan@crossbowstudio.com

DON'T SELL ME, TELL ME

61958828R00088

Made in the USA
Lexington, KY
24 March 2017